See It, Say It, Seize It . . . It's Yours

See It, Say It, Seize It . . . It's Yours

By: Don H. Polson

See It, Say It, Seize It . . . It's Yours

www.donhpolston.com
The Life That Wins, Inc. ®

ISBN 978-0-557-68043-6

Printed in the United States of America

All Scripture citations are from the *King James Version* of the Bible.

Order books by Don H. Polston
www.donhpolston.com

The Law of Faith . . . Wins
See It, Say It, Seize It . . . It's Yours
Like Yourself Unconditionally
The Life That Wins . . . Yes!
Living Without Losing . . . Really
There Can Be a New You . . . Today
Be More Than You Are . . . It's Possible
Where There's a Wall, There's a Way . . . Always
Tears on the Soul . . . Refreshing
The Need Stimulates . . . to Action
Inspirational Strategies . . . Straight Ahead
Life's Battles Are Winnable
The Force of Faith . . . Creating
The Road to Healing . . . Step by Step
What Has Separated Your Heart? . . . Find It Again
Start Talking Faith as You Understand It

Editorial Note

I believe it is helpful to say a few words about the style and punctuation in *See It, Say It, Seize It . . . It's Yours.* Most significantly, Polston establishes a unique rhythmic and spatial style. It is important to stay true to the *feel* that he wishes to express.

Thus, the effort here is to preserve the character of Polston's use of rhythm and space; stylistic aspects regarding paragraph lengths, or the use of capitalization and italicization, are in line with Polston's intuitive preferences.

For example: Polston also likes to use commas—even where one might not usually expect—in order to create a short and thoughtful pause in the reading.

In addition, Polston has a unique way of utilizing and/or creating technical terms. Some of these are compounds which he tends to place in italics, especially when first introduced—Such compounds are usually two words linked with a hyphen, e.g., faith-seed. Sometimes such a compound is placed in quotation marks, e.g., "faith-cell." Also, occasionally a word or compound is capitalized in order to bring extra attention to it. Of course, any word meant to draw special attention is italicized.

Furthermore, scriptural reference is placed within parentheses without the verse(s) being provided—it is the author's intention in these cases for the reader to look up the verse(s) him/herself.

Contents

Briefing

Life is not simple. The waves of change, challenge, and danger swoop into our doors like a tsunami. We can run from difficulties, deny their existence, face them head-on for answers, or let them eventually consume us.

No one escapes the war on the soul or the war on life. At times, you have to fight.

The battle to win and to understand the minute conflicts of the soul and come through them wiser and a winner is the purpose of life. It's really in your port of call.

The success you seek is in your struggles. The tensions of life are used to keep you awake to the possibilities in your life. Tensions strengthen your understanding.

In this book, you will learn about the dangers and defeats of inner conflicts, outer conflicts, and how to emerge a winner. The truth in this book is not for the satisfied or the uncourageous. Only brave souls examine details.

Don't let unknown, unseen, or unsolved struggles consume you. Get into the fight for victorious living.

Search each chapter for hidden answers. Crossing the sea is dangerous. It takes strength. It takes time. And it takes faith to launch out and find new worlds.

Let's get started in our self-discovery, faith discovery, and finally, our God discovery. Read a chapter a day. Digest it. Think on it. Talk about it. And finally, work it out in your daily walk.

PART ONE

When the Devil Sees You

Can it be true that when the devil sees you, he is seeing someone who looks like Christ—who is crucified and resurrected? Can the transformation, the metamorphosis of Christ's nature, be that real? Yes!

The transformation is a supernatural upgrade.

The Spirit of metamorphosis is changing one nature into another nature, with a complete exchange of natures. In addition, it is functioning as if it was magical. The higher element is affecting the lower element, removing or replacing it altogether with a new element.

The work of the Holy Spirit in your inner man is so vital that the devils hardly recognize you as you.

You are becoming as your Lord, even though it is a process. Think about it. In a matter of a few years, you are fashioned in image and in nature as Jesus. That is swift! That is awesome!

When the Enemy hits you, he is hitting Jesus. When people bless you, they are blessing Jesus. The only evidence of who you are is external. However, the internal is the nature of Christ formed in you.

Jesus prayed that we would be one with the Father (see John 17:21-23). "I in them, and thou in me, that they may be made perfect in one; that the world may know that thou has sent me, and hast loved them, as thou hast loved Me." That is quite a prayer!

The purpose of redemption is to restore the inner man to a union with God through the operations of the Holy Spirit. This glory or union is the very dignity of the Godhead Spirit in you.

Act like it. Think like it. There is no greater spirit of humility and holiness than to know you are a carrier of God in your spirit. There is little need for external law once you believe the internal law. It is naturally, supernaturally, fixed in you.

At this point, grow into the knowledge of that Law. Instinctively, you will know and live the life of Christ.

All Natures Respond Naturally

If you have the nature of something, then you can be assured that it will respond to any stimulus that appeals to that nature. The Spirit's purpose in you, then, is to develop to the fullest the very nature of Christ. He will never give up until you respond to the world, the flesh, and the devil as the nature of Christ responds.

One can train a nature, but one cannot implant a nature. There is no way, through the teachings of the church, to implant the nature of Christ in a person.

The purpose of the Church is to enlarge and ignite that nature through the knowledge of the Word and the demonstrations of the Spirit. Here is the "rest" that belongs to the people of God. You have ceased seeking to live like Christ by the efforts of the flesh or the human. In your flesh dwells no good thing.

You will always have your likes, dislikes, struggles, and many other human responses while Christ is living His life through you.

When God lives His life through you and as you, He sends you into the world as healer, rescuer, and restorer. Paul's prayer is that you may be complete and perfect in the nature of Christ (see 1 Corinthians 4:12). To be complete is to be crammed full and imbued with the very life of Christ.

To be perfect is to be who the Spirit created you to be. A baseball may not be perfect, but it is still a baseball. It was designed to be a baseball, not a bat. You were designed to be full of God, "...that you might be filled with all the fullness of God" (Ephesians 3:19). In this sense, you are a perfect person in process.

There is much work for the Spirit, the church, and your own walk of faith to do to accomplish this goal. Renewing the mind, teaching new ways of life, and replacing the old ways is a monumental task!

However, if you don't give up, the Spirit will continue His work in you! He will finish the work He began.

The Spirit of the Mind

Ephesians 4:23 says, "…be renewed in the spirit of your mind." The word renewed means to "renovate."

We are told that Jesus renovated a man who was filled with some six thousand devils. It is said, "...the man, out of whom the devils were departed, was sitting at the feet of Jesus, in his right mind: and they were afraid" (Luke 8:35).

It is interesting to note that this man, who had some six thousand demons, was now clothed and sitting at the feet of Jesus in his right mind. This caused fear among the people. They were more afraid of the man in his right mind than the man in his demonic or wrong mind. Being in his wrong mind or demonic mind was acceptable.

The mind is the center of your being. How it is affected affects the whole life.

The spirit of the mind is different from the brain.

You can have a brain without a mind. The very first step of Satan is to catch the mind. This is also Christ's first step. Catching the mind, filling the mind, and renewing the mind are the works of the Holy Spirit. They lead to all of life.

There are some ninety-five times the word "mind" is found in the Bible. Here are a few:

> "…neither be ye of doubtful of mind" (Luke 12:29, emphasis mine).

> "…God gave them over to a reprobate mind" (Romans 1:28).

> "…transformed by the renewing of your mind" (Romans 12:1).

> "…for if there be first a willing mind, it is accepted" (2 Corinthians 8:12).

> "…let this mind be in you, which was also in Christ Jesus" (Philippians 2:5).

"…I beseech Euodias, and beseech Syntyche, that they be of the same mind in the Lord" (Philippians 4:2).

"…That ye be not soon shaken in mind, or be troubled" (2 Thessalonians 2:2).

"…for God hath not given us the spirit of fear; but of power, and of love, and of a sound mind" (2 Timothy 1:7).

Following a meeting, a woman said to me, "When I realized that the mind is spirit, I was instantly changed on the inside. I am totally a new person. I saw the need for God to change the spirit of my mind. That fact altered me completely. I am a new person in thought and action."

The tyranny of the old mind needs the replacement by the new mind.

Replacing the Subconscious Thoughts

Ephesians 3:16 declares, with regard to the inner mind or the subconscious, that one would "...be strengthened with might by his Spirit in the inner man..." The inner mind is the subconscious.

The tyranny of the old, subconscious mind needs replacement by a new, triumphant, subconscious mind. The subconscious is the storage place for what has been experienced—good or bad. These experiences produce images, feelings, and memories. The work of the Spirit is to replace the old bad images with fresh, uplifting new images and memories.

What you see in your mind is where you go and what you become.

The tyrannical or the triumphant life starts in the mind.

Nothing can replace these images, visions, or habits in the mind but the Spirit of the Lord. Here is the urgency to renew the mind. Renew has the idea of replacing, removing, and refreshing the mind. The process of renewing the mind is threefold: (1) the Spirit of the Word, (2) the anointing of the Word, and (3) acting on the fact of the Word.

Only the enlightened Word replaces the wounded word. The Holy Spirit replaces the broken human spirit.

In fact, the whole of life is spirit. Everything flows out of and into your spirit. The whole universe moves on spirit or light. Whatever spirit dominates wins the day. God said, "I will pour out of my Spirit" (Acts 2:17). Why? Because the Spirit was poured out and is being poured out to dominate the spirit of death, disease, war, and evil. The Spirit is not only the igniter of the universe, but it is also the cleanser of the universe . . . your personal universe.

The reason there is a conflict between the conscious and the subconscious mind is that the Spirit is replacing, casting down, and casting out the old, inner images with greater and newer images in the growing person. There will always be this conflict. The conflict between flesh and Spirit is the conflict of the Spirit casting down the subconscious response to old thoughts.

God is building a new person. He is implanting the winning idea. The overcoming person is the designed one, by His hand—realized in true life.

Deleting Old Images

Many images in the subconscious mind need deleting. However, there are other images in the subconscious mind or the inner man that do not only need deleting, but also developing. It appears that deleting and developing the mind go side by side in the process.

This is the process of being "…cleansed with the washing of water by the word…" (Ephesians 5:26). The Word tells us that the Spirit cleanses and deletes the old neurotic guilt or neurotic thoughts and addicted patterns. Many of these neurotic tendencies have risen from your first days—the first years of seeking to follow a strict set of self-imposed rules (thinking it was the Spirit's imposition).

In time, you will be set free from these old patterns of thought and conduct. The reason the subconscious mind and the conscious mind are in conflict, as stated above, is that the Spirit is replacing the old images in the deep, inner mind and emotions while, at the same time, teaching and implanting new ideas and new images in the new, regenerated mind.

The Spirit is deleting the old ways—sending them to the recycle bin. In time, it will become very difficult to recall the old sins and disappointments that have kept you in fear and bondage. You are dead to the old images and alive to the new images. The dying is a process, blurring the images of defeat and fear.

Conscious desires—human desires—are in conflict with subconscious red lights or green lights. There is as much danger of having too many subconscious red lights as there is with having too many subconscious green lights. The neurotic—the one who has not understood the power of replacement or right of passage—exaggerates and aggravates one or the other.

Because of this ignorance, the neurotic—out of weakness of conscience or the need to please—surrenders to the unlearned and undeveloped subconscious demands, thereby becoming a greater slave.

Walking in the Spirit is virtually impossible until the subconscious or the inner man is filled and illuminated by the Spirit.

One keeps stumbling over good intentions until the deep, inner mind or the subconscious is cleared up by the Spirit's illumination with greater knowledge.

When the inner man is free, the whole life is spontaneous. There is a light and joy about the free inner person expressed outwardly.

Little by little, you are learning to let the old, defeated struggles find their way into the recycle bin. The more you know of Jesus, the better you follow and the better you understand the life of faith.

Walking in the Spirit is freedom. The bondage is being deleted.

Paul declared, "For the law of the Spirit of life in Christ Jesus hath made me free from the law of sin and death" (Romans 8:2).

You can judge if you have found this freedom by the number of bondages that hold you.

Are you free? Free from all—except the bondage of love?

Living in a Greater Awareness

You are a spirit-person, learning to live from the inner source while also learning to live life in the natural.

To live from the inner man—the inner source—demands a realistic remembrance of when the transaction took place. It has its Pentecost moment or time where the transaction took place. This transaction became the ideal for all movement—working and walking in the natural—while at the same time working and walking in the spiritual. You moved from simply being a natural man into being a spirit-man. The hidden secret is now known to you.

The secret of success—the secret of overcoming the struggles and stress—is to live out from the inner man. The inner man has a higher consciousness. There is now a greater enlightenment—a greater ignition—meant for vigorous living. It is "to be strengthened with might by his Spirit in the inner man" (Ephesians 3:16).

To have the might of the Spirit in the inner man is to have miraculous power and marvelous ability—living in abundance of the Spirit's flow.

The power or ability to walk with Christ means having this vital reality become conscious within you. However, consciousness is not feelings. It goes much deeper than feelings. There is a silent light within—a steady force—a winning awareness without seeing the winning every time. It knows it is a winner, even in the event of losing. Losing is only a temporary setback for a greater comeback.

Although you are a human-person, you are learning to walk as a spirit-person. You are in the human, but ever learning to allow the anointed human spirit, in the inner man, to lead, to take control, and to carry out business transactions without coming out of the inner source.

Once you are born again and filled with the Holy Spirit (as a second experience following conversion), you are conscious of the human and the inner divine working as one. There will be times when this factor seems in conflict. However, the conflict is only a method of birthing new insights, gaining new truths, and finding new paths to leadership. It is the new inner man, serving in newness of spirit and not walking in the oldness of the letter or the old man. He has imparted to you all He is. It is up to you to seek it out and work it out in your daily life. You are responsible for this process.

You no longer walk in the "vanity of your mind" (Ephesians 4:17). The vanity mind is full of futility, folly, emptiness, and darkness. You are learning to walk in the unity of the mind, no longer following the double-minded patterns. The vanity has given way to unity.

The subconscious is learning to be dominated by the mind of the inner man. The inner mind is learning from the mind of Christ.

Are you still in the glorious pursuit learning how His mind works for you and works through you?

The Right Mind

"…the man, out of whom the devils were departed, [was] sitting at the feet of Jesus, clothed, and in his right mind" (Luke 8:35).

This man lost the use of his right mind. He no longer had control over his thoughts, and this was affecting his emotions. He did not lose his brain, but he lost the correct use of his brain. Before Jesus touched him, the mind was unsound. Devils had possessed his unsound mind.

The brain is a substance—an organic substance—but the mind is not organic. The mind is spirit—able to be anywhere, anytime. The brain can sleep, but the mind never sleeps. The Holy Spirit possesses the mind of the faith-person, and devils possess the mind of the evil person. The degree the Spirit or the Devil possesses the mind is up to the individual's surrender and knowledge.

There is a right mind and a wrong mind. The wrong mind is out of control. The thoughts are blurred and unsteady. It has lost the ability to be discreet. The wrong mind has difficulty being temperate. There is little self-control in the wrong mind.

The right mind is consistent—steady. It is dependable. The right mind is a gift of God. It is free from the spirit of fear or the overreactions to the ordinary ways of living.

The fearful mind sees the matters or issues of life out of focus. It has a dominant thought that leaves the person or the mind in turmoil. The one dominant thought affects the whole of life. The fearful mind cannot move beyond its own boundaries. It feels safe in its prison of thought.

But the demon possessed man who Jesus healed was in his right mind!

The noble mind—the sound mind—acts honorably and according to rank. It is aware when things are out of place. The noble mind needs little restrictions socially, matrimonially, or ecclesiastically. It knows.

The greater you seek to control the inner man, the inner mind, or the subconscious, without the Spirit's anointing, the greater you build up resistance and rebellion. Restrictions without revelation lead to rebellion of the worst sort.

The law, even good laws, builds resistance when not done in the power and gentleness of the Spirit. The law may restrain, but it cannot replace the nature. It is impossible to train the old man—the old nature—without the touch of the Holy Spirit. If one cannot tame the tongue, how much more can one *not* tame the nature? The nature does not need to be tamed; it needs to be replaced by a greater Nature.

Seeking to create an image of a Christian, without the indwelling of Christ's Spirit, creates more evil. The only answer for such a dilemma is a replacement.

I had crippling pain in my right hip until I had it replaced. This same fact holds true for the inner man. There are not enough tranquilizers to tame this inner mind. Tranquilizers affect the brain, but they cannot reach the depth of the inner man or the inner mind. The inner mind not only needs tranquilizing at times, but it also needs a transfusion at all times with the Spirit of the living God.

One mighty touch of the Holy Spirit and that uncontrolled mind, uncontrolled attitude, or uncontrolled emotion is brought under the dominance of the Spirit's sound mind.

What hope!

Creative Thoughts vs. Destructive Thoughts

Thoughts are real things. Thoughts are constructive and they are also destructive.

A nation can fall in a matter of a few years by being bombarded with hateful thoughts. Self-destructive thoughts or self-distractive thoughts will defeat anyone. Your spirit is real. Real effects come from the spirit through the mind to the world, affecting your environment.

Thoughts are energy. Not being able to see a thing does not mean it does not exist. Thoughts are energetic. They are electric movers. They can electrify or electrocute.

If you are in a place of evil thoughts, then you will feel the thoughts, and in time, you will accept them as vital. If you are in the presence of thoughts of defeat, where others are expressing or speaking defeated thoughts, then you will feel defeated and depressed. Walk into a prison or a hospital and feel the effects.

"Let no corrupt communication proceed out of your mouth," is not a restriction; it is releasing of life (Ephesians 4:29). Paul warned, "...Be not deceived: evil communications corrupt good manners" (1 Corinthians 15:33).

On the other hand, creative thoughts and expressions of faith or hope build up a people. Paul termed it "edifying one another" (1 Thessalonians 5:11). Edifying has the idea of confirming, approving, and accepting each other. Be careful of associating with those who are putting you down, belittling your efforts, or ignoring your accomplishments. This type of association erodes your confidence instead of edifying it.

You are constantly being surrounded by destructive thoughts from the printed press, high definition television news, and the stranded church. Choose the people and the places that make you feel accepted, and be fully enabled and aggressive in your faith and work.

If you want smart thoughts, hang around smart people.

If you desire holy thoughts, stay around the godly. If you want the anointing, then associate with anointed people.

If you want a greater nation, then speak well of its people, its government, and its success. If you want a greater church, do the same. If you want outstanding children, tell them how marvelous they are. If you want a sweeter wife or a more thoughtful husband, express your encouragement and approval to them. Try it for thirty days. It works.

Thoughts do create. What are you creating in your world by your thoughts? What you think, you seek.

PART TWO

Strong Thoughts

Your thoughts must be stronger than your enemy's thoughts (devils or people), or you will stumble in the pursuit of your goals. Your faith must be more vigorous—keenly stronger than the unbelief surrounding you—or you will catch the spirit of unbelief.

Your imagination is developing your mind—squeezing it into a viable shape and molding it into a fixed pattern of thought and conduct. What primary imagination is squeezing you into its form? Whatever the mind is fixed on fixes the thought into action. Whoever has the greatest thought wins.

It is declared that the thoughts and imaginations of the human heart are evil. "And God saw that the wickedness of man was great in the earth, and that every imagination of the thoughts of his heart was only evil continually" (Genesis 6:5).

When dealing with a pressing need or a troubling situation, your spirit must be more dynamic than the need, or you will catch the disease in the troubling situation. The need will entrench your world instead of you entrenching it.

Whoever has the greatest need to win, wins.

You must have strong, focused thoughts if you are to win over the thoughts of a troubling world. The world thinks in thoughts of fear, utter impossibilities, expectant failure, and scorching scorn. People will stumble when they have destructive thoughts about themselves.

Anyone can be defeated if thoughts of defeat are injected and accepted in the mind. Any untrue statement said about you, if accepted, will lead you to the very snare the statement inferred. Your mind must be shielded, but expanding as you move about in society.

We are told to "bless and not curse" in Romans 12:14. When you bless or encourage another, and they accept the praise or encouragement as true, then they immediately start to move in the direction of the blessing. On the other hand, if you curse or denounce another, and they accept it, then they will start to move in the direction of the curse. To curse another is to declare them to be detestable.

Start blessing yourself, your home, and your business. Prophesy over your own life with good words. What you bless increases! (And what you curse increases, too.) What are you blessing?

Invading Thoughts

Thoughts are floating throughout the universe—ever seeking to invade your mind for the purpose of controlling, influencing and directing your affairs.

The thoughts of prayer, peace, and despair are seeking to invade your mind. Where you live will affect your daily thoughts. You must decide what will enter your mind or your imagination, for out of your mind precede actions that equal the thought.

Words are thoughts. You cannot speak a word without a thought.

When you hide the enlightened Word in your heart, it turns to motivating thoughts. And the thoughts turn to expressions. What you think about is what you talk about. And what you talk about is what you take on as true.

The Bible says that out of the heart proceeds evil thought (Matthew 15:19). The word "evil" in the original refers to harmful or hurtful thoughts. Guard your mind from entertaining thoughts or memories that are harmful and hurtful to your peace.

Words spoken to you with fearful limitations or words spoken with hate sink into the subconscious of the inner man's mind as thoughts; later, as you start toward your goals, these thoughts emerge as roadblocks, stymieing your vision and holding your emotions in bondage. These invading thoughts, perhaps at a time of childhood or in times of crises, start pouring out in torrents—affecting your present pursuit and peace.

When the inner man is full of untrue thoughts, it results in bondage-producing emotions. You feel normal in your soul-pain or your limited circumstances if misguided thoughts were injected into your mind. Paul urges you to cast down these imaginations and every high thing that exalts itself against the knowledge of Christ (2 Corinthians 10:5).

If you are cast down, it is because you are not casting down these imaginations or hurtful thoughts. Nevertheless, there is comfort for those who are cast down.

Paul declares, "Nevertheless, God, which comforteth those that are cast down, comforted us by the coming of Titus" (2 Corinthians 7:6). The word "comfort" does not mean coziness, but one being cheered on by another—one being exhorted to keep running the race. How is this accomplished? In Paul's situation, by the coming of Titus to him. The comforting of your spirit is found in the cheering of your comrades—the faith-cheerers. Titus was a faith-bringer to Paul. Are you a faith-cheerer or a faith-crusher?

The woman doctor looked at us over the lunch booth and said, "When I was four, I had made a little table of tea for my brothers. I called my older brothers to come and have some tea with me in my little teacups. I was only playing teatime. In my mind, there was no tea, only fun teatime. When my father found this out, he scolded me harshly and said, "You lied. You are lying to offer tea to your brothers when you knew there was no tea in those cups."

She continued her story and explained, "From that day on, I never could buy jewelry, put makeup on, or act out my girlish ways without severe guilt. Even in my adult years, I could never put on makeup without feeling guilty. It took years and good counseling to free me from some of these old guilt feelings, which came from my father's words that day long ago." Today she is a successful physician, but she still works with those old guilt feelings.

Someone of authority and value crushed the heart of this tender child and nearly perverted her little girlish ways to self-destruction. But today she is an accomplished medical doctor and a deep believer in the power of the Spirit's deliverance. Someone's faith-cheers are helping to make her whole.

Are you cheering someone to maturity?

Normal in Soul Pain?

You can be very sincere in your values, but if your thoughts are built on untruth, then they will produce emotional bondage, which hinders your vocation, your prayers, your vision, and your marriage. You feel normal in spirit-pain, mind-turmoil, and limited circumstances if this is true. The image you have of yourself will be the acceptance of your situation as normal. The only way to change the situation or the circumstance is to change the self-image. Self-doubt has a high price tag.

How you see yourself is how you project yourself, and how you protect yourself.

You have accepted the present irritating limitations in your life because you accepted these restricted thoughts. Even though you recognize that you are being defeated and held by these negative thoughts, you allowed the pattern to continue because it feels right for you. Regardless of its effects on your general life pattern, your vocation, or your spiritual walk, you allowed this trend to continue.

However, you must take charge of your thoughts (regarding who you are and what you are) if you are to have a healthy self-image.

It is not pride to say to yourself, "I am smart. I am able. I am loved. I am adequate, and I am successful. I am anointed. I am a believer. I am a good father, or a good mother and a good partner." The Apostle Paul declared, "I can do all things…through Christ who strengthens me" (Philippians 4:13). Paul is saying, "I am able and enabled by Christ to do all things sufficiently." Let this become your speech, your imagination, and your new lifestyle, too.

Once you are enlightened, you must then learn new ways and form new habits by taking a steady control of your conscious thinking pattern. In time, you will replace the old, negative, fearful, and unhappy thoughts. Renew, rewind, and refresh your mind in prayer, in Bible reading, and in fellowshipping with Spirit-positive people. Replacement is a process of renewal.

Your prayers become stronger, more intense, and more expectant when your thoughts are stronger and more focused. As you pray in the

Holy Spirit, many times your thoughts are inexpressible, but the inner images of your prayer requests are more vivid. You see clearly what you are not able to express clearly, because you have replaced the old defeated images with the new Spirit-implanted images.

Now you not only pray, but you see the answers in your inner eye. This is the single eye because it has a single mind. The mind is full of light. The soul-pain is no longer normal for you (Luke 11:34).

What do you need to replace to find release?

The Intuitive Mind

The purpose of the anointed mind is to see—to perceive what is beyond the apparent. Anyone can see or perceive what is visible or in appearance, but only the Spirit-anointed mind is able to apprehend what is beyond appearance. This faith-mind is looking through appearances.

We are told, "...judge not according to appearances" (1 John 7:24). The faith-mind—the Spirit-intuitive mind—looks not at what is seen, but what is unseen. It was said of Jesus, "...He perceived in His spirit that they reasoned within themselves" (Mark 2:8). It was also said of the Apostle Paul, that "...a man, impotent in his feet... [and Paul] steadfastly beholding him, perceived that he had faith to be healed, [and] said in a loud voice, Stand upright on thy feet. And he leaped and walked" (Acts 14:8-10).

Paul exercised this intuitive mind and perceived that another individual had faith to be healed! When Paul called out this fact, the faith of the man was rewarded in healing. Blessed are the people who have association with others who have this anointing of perception. Many needs go unmet because no one is discerning the faith or the need in another.

There was a movement in the early 1900's called "surrealism," which means "super-realism." It seeks to know a higher reality than that of the daily, natural life. However, the Spirit-anointed believer has known this surrealism for centuries. The super-realism is faith. The Spirit intuitive mind is seeing beyond what is apparent in the natural. It sees beyond the daily, ordinary situations. The believer is walking in a higher reality. He actually is looking down—back from the throne of God into the world where he walks and lives. The Spirit's endowment and unction unfolds the darkness of the age, uncovers the hidden workings of Satan, and stands on the unseen footsteps of God.

You need this intuitive mind of the Spirit to succeed in business, to lead your family, to be useful in the work of God, and to influence your generation. Walking in darkness and confusion is not God's ideal.

He desires for you to walk as light, in the light, and to have the light to shine on all your endeavors.

Is your intuitive mind illuminated?

Reason and Revelation

The perceptive mind goes beyond reason. However, reason undergirds the perceptive mind. The two work as one in the enlightened person.

The apostles James, Cephas, and John had this double ability when they interviewed Paul and Barnabas. Paul analyzed, "…[they] perceived the grace that was given unto me, and they gave to me and Barnabas the right hand of fellowship" (Galatians 2:9).

The apostles discerned that perceptive grace was given to these new apostles. It resulted in widening the fellowship and the mighty out reach of the church. Actually, it resulted in the establishment of the New Testament. Out of the twenty-six letters in the New Testament, Paul penned about thirteen of them. What if the first apostles had failed to recognize the perceptive grace in these two new men?

How much is lost in the church because leadership fails to recognize the grace of God and the gifting of grace on the new "apostles"? Reasoning alone could not have perceived this grace in Paul and Barnabas. In fact, if the three leaders had depended on reasoning alone, they would have rejected both Paul and Barnabas.

If the church leads by reasoning alone (committees, sessions) and fails to avail itself of this perception ability (using not only the mind, but also the Spirit) then much time is wasted and the movement of God is frustrated. Paul said he would not frustrate the grace of God. In other words, "I do not neutralize the grace of God" (see Galatians 2:21).

When the church functions on rationality alone, it fails to understand the value of another and the needs of others.

There may be the need for healing or salvation, yet these needs go unmet because there is a lack of the anointing to discern the need. The Spirit anointing gives the ability to "read" the intent, the faith, or the grace in another.

The tendency, instead, is to turn to dialogue (exchanging ideas regarding a matter) instead of knowing what the mind of the Spirit on a matter is. It is reasoning without revelation.

The scribes were reasoning in their hearts concerning Jesus. They were literally dialoging and musing among themselves. This type of thinking led to the crucifixion of Jesus. Dialoging with the devil or doubts leads to destruction. You don't dialogue with evil; resist it.

If the rational mind is not tied to the revelational mind, then you have error; on the other hand, if the revelational mind is not tied to the reasoning mind, then you have fanaticism. Paul said he would use his mind and work with his spirit also (1 Corinthians 14:15). A safe way to go.

Are you working with the reasoning or rational mind, plus the revelational or Spirit enlightened mind on the matter facing you today? This is your secret in finding life-changing answers.

PART THREE

Unfounded Fears

When you are being held by unfounded fears, with an overly sensitive conscience to the voice of the Spirit or the voice of Satan, as well as the voice of self, it becomes increasingly more difficult to distinguish which voice is to be obeyed.

If Satan knows your secret fear of an object, or your fear of an action, then he uses it to leave you in condemnation and confusion. If he accomplishes this tactic, then he has won a victory over you in that part of your life.

Hebrews 5:14 instructs, if you are to learn the difference between good and evil, that, "…strong meat belongeth to them that are of full age, even those who by reason of use have their senses [good judgment] exercised [practice] to discern both good and evil."

The estimation of a thing is only gained as the senses are in use—without a cover up. Practicing naked-mindedness, while using good judgment to gain a full estimation of a situation, is one of the safest ways to distinguish the proper voices.

The senses of the Spirit-filled are keenly made aware of truth by searching, comparing, hearing, or by feeling as one who is unclothed in mind seeking the truth. There is no preconceived blanket over the mind while searching for the truth.

Let's follow a young man who overcame his phobias.

Phobias in Learning to Walk with God

Phobias come in many forms. The fear of the past, mistakes in the present, and carryovers from youth to adulthood all may cast a tormenting spell over your emotions because of a phobic reaction. The contradictions, imposed convictions, or self-imposed restrictions all create unfounded fears and phobias, which make it doubly difficult to keep your walk steady or your inner feelings at peace.

I knew a young man (I'll call him Jimmy) who suffered from great fears and self-imposed phobias. He was committed to doing everything perfectly, keeping every "might be sinful" thing out of his life. This caused anxiety and neurotic tendencies, though at the same time he has a fervent commitment to walk with God.

He also refused the desire of the natural—the sexual desires—from his teen years up to his twenties. He refused to express any sexual emotions. And because of his stern discipline, all sexual responses or expressions were stopped. Never touching himself sexually became a stern restriction. It became a fixed fear that touching himself was sinful, and it displeased God. And the amazing thing is that, according to Jimmy, he actually accomplished it.

There was no contact with girls all through his teens. He never knew a girl romantically or affectionately until he was in his early twenties. These restrictions seemed to be an honorable accomplishment at the time. However, it was setting him up for deep emotional pain and confusion after marriage.

After marriage, all those old fears, restrictions, and stern disciplines became neuroses in his married life. These sexual restrictions came to the surface to torment him after having sexual expressions in marriage.

The old fear of touching himself held him in marriage as much as when he was single. Even sexual touching from his wife became a stern restriction in his mind. The road ahead was filled with pitfalls. The anxiety of displeasing God, as he walked through the teen years, now followed him into his adult married years. What was wrong back then could not be removed from his conscious responses now. It was hell.

Let's learn more from this young man. Read on regarding ignorant emotions.

Dealing with Unfounded, Ignorant Emotions

The sexual emotions that were rejected in youth by Jimmy became the same sexual restrictions for him as an adult married man. The attempt to accept his sexual expressions that were rejected in youth carried the same emotion of shame in marriage. It was all a carry-over-idea or concept that needed to be understood and released.

Apostle Paul expressed it like this in Romans 8:15, "For ye have not received the spirit of bondage again to fear…" Whatever holds you in the spirit of fear or the spirit of bondage, no matter how right it seems, is not the spirit of faith or the spirit of adoption.

It was almost impossible for Jimmy to move from no sex, restrained for years, into the freedom of sex. The old mind-images could not be completely reversed from the old restrictions to the new releases. It was a battle of faith—a battle of understanding—to reverse these tormenting emotions.

These unfounded emotions had to be desensitized if he was going to be out of reach of these troubling emotions. The fears had to be unlearned. He had to be delivered from this spirit of shame.

At one time in life, the restrictions seemed admirable. But later in life they were destructive to peace and happiness. Being frozen in time is being frozen in emotions. Both are unhealthy. Jimmy was frozen in time and emotions.

It will take courage and trust in the love of God, and self-trust, to break out of the frozen state to a life of liberty and joy. Jimmy gradually confronted each of his fears, desensitizing himself little by little until he finally broke out of his own imprisonment.

Nevertheless, the tormenting demon or the tormenting emotions are not far out of reach. They return to reclaim the ground Jimmy took in his search for freedom. He needs to rehearse the freedom repeatedly until the oppressive spirits cannot accuse or abuse.

Tormenting demons use any crisis or emotional weakness to trouble the sensitive soul. Nearly every unhealthy emotional problem that holds you can be traced to a weakness in some area of your life. We must not be ignorant of the devices and tricks that camouflage the voice of Satan as the voice of the Spirit. Paul shouted, "… lest Satan should get an advantage of us… for we are not ignorant of his devices" (2 Corinthians 2:11).

Satan is not interested in you being holy. He will use the holiness standard or a sinless standard to dog your steps by his devices to keep you in uncertainty. In this way, he hopes to drive you to despair and uselessness. All mental tormenting makes one useless to God and to others.

To be ignorant of Satan's devices is to give him the power to overreach. Don't let him do it. Find someone who will cast that spirit of torment out of you and uncover the deception.

Jimmy kept searching for truth regarding these tormenting feelings. He is in the process of reclaiming his freedom. Time will tell if he has made the transaction successfully.

Satan Uses the Good to Control You

We have seen the struggles in Jimmy's life resulting from good intentions and strong restraints. Here is what I learned from being with Jimmy and many others:

1. Don't let the devil tell you what it is to be righteous. He knows nothing of truth of what it is to be holy or how to please God. There is no truth in him at all.

2. Don't allow the devil to teach you how to live in action or conduct. He only leads as "an angel of light" to bring confusion and darkness. If he cannot get you to sin, then he makes what you do seem like sin in your mind. It is well to remember this fact when dealing with your walk of purity and useful living.

3. Don't take instructions from satanic spirits in how to live the Christian life. Satan doesn't care about your holiness. He is only interested in tying you up in restrictions, so that it becomes impossible to fulfill his irritating law.

There are three classes of believers that Satan seeks to deceive while they seek for more of God:

(1) The immature
(2) The ignorant
(3) The deeply sensitive

(1) The immature are led to believe that the more they are austere, the more holy and devout they will become. They think that submitting to rules, ordinances, and dogmatism regarding the satisfying of the body will bring them into a closer relationship to Christ.

Being immature, they are led into a false concept of holiness, which, in time, becomes impossible to maintain, and thereby, they become self-righteous with self-imposed restrictions. The false concept must be uncovered. It is taking the risk to find your true self in relation to God's desire. The reward is worth the risk. Every misconception of a thing leads to greater ignorance of the thing.

(2) The ignorant are those who have no knowledge of how demons work. Demons seek to get the ignorant to submit to principles that promise freedom and power but produce more bondage and confusion.

This is "will worship," which is the worship of austerity and the sanctimonious image. People innocently are led to commitments and covenants, which demons know they will not be able to keep, thereby using it against their self-image and aggressiveness for Christ.

The ignorant believer becomes like the Pharisees, who, in the beginning, had good intentions of keeping the law, but ended up being harsh, judgmental, and rejected by the Lord. They were a poor image of His grace.

(3) The deeply devout or the deeply sensitive are the most open to deception. The deeply sensitive are open to the most tormenting restrictions. Each time they enjoy natural pleasures, they feel condemned. They quickly give up to the inner guilt pressures and seek peace at any cost.

This method leads to self-condemnation, because they are not able to keep the mind from some form of condemnation or guilt while enjoying the natural, legitimate pleasures. In this misunderstanding, it seems they feel unworthy most of the time, thereby restricting themselves from boldness in prayer and a witness for Christ.

The result is an emotional, spiritual wimp.

Their strong image has been lost because of giving in or giving up to the demanding voice of the enemy; yet it was the voice of the enemy cutting into their deeply sensitive heart. The purpose of the enemy was to control their mental and emotional life, thereby controlling their faith.

Are you involved in this type of spiritual confusion? Seek a way out immediately. Ask God to lead you to a trusted friend for counseling and prayer. Deliverance from these tormenting spirits is a must if you are to live a happy and victorious life.

Do the Thing You Fear

Unfounded fears lead to hardness, cynicism, and self-rejection.

If you are being held captive by phobias or unfounded constrictions, then your life will be filled with worries and torments. Seldom will you sense the sweet presence and deep approval of God in your heart if you are held captive by unfounded fears. Satan seeks to use what once was a good principle and turn it into a ball and chain around your mind. The dreams you held at one time are lost in the nightmares of walking a path of uncertainty.

At this point of your life, you need someone anointed to recognize your struggles and give you the rite of passage or permission to be who you are. The rite of passage is vital if you are to survive and enjoy freedom in Christ.

It is virtually impossible to free others in their struggles if you are not free yourself. Understanding yourself causes you to better understand God's dealings and to minister to others. Understanding is the path to acting and living with joy. In most cases, if you understand your struggles then you can overcome them.

Do the thing you fear, and fear will lose its hold on you.

Face your fears with courage—with an expectation to win over them. To face a fear will take inner strength. You will feel, at times, as if you are all alone in the battle with these old phobias. Your fears are a learned response to an action or a situation you thought was true. All harmful responses must be unlearned if they are a hindrance to your well-being.

Gradually expose your fears to truth, honesty, and adventure. Take the time to examine the fear to see if it is true for you at this point of your life, or if it holds you in self-doubt toward yourself and toward God. If the fear makes you feel less human, less mature, or less bold, then cast it off. Dare to challenge it.

How would you feel if you knew the thing you feared was not true? How would you act if you suddenly found out that the fear or phobia came out of your own mind? What would you do if you discovered the truth about your fears? Make the attempt to find out.

Seeking freedom has the approval of God. Are you seeking?

Desensitize

You must learn how to desensitize yourself to an action of fear if you are to enjoy life and your walk with God. The Apostle Paul expressed it this way: "Happy is he that condemneth not himself in that thing which he alloweth. He that doubts is condemned; because what is not of faith is sin" (Romans 14:22-23).

The reason for your fear is based on the hesitating attempt or the hesitating assumption causing you to waver in your decision. The more detailed the matter called into question, the greater the fear. You need to desensitize the details and focus on the wholeness of your life, devoted to God.

Learn how to challenge the thing in question. You must examine or search for the truth regarding the situation while refusing to waver or hesitate in your choice. Desensitizing takes time; trust in your own heart or motives for the method of desensitizing to work.

Only you know the reason and the desire for the desensitizing. If it has caused you much pain, much confusion, and mental anguish, then it needs desensitizing. Confusion is not of God. He does not lead in confusing ways. He leads in clarity, wholeness, and in well-being.

His people should be the most balanced people in the world. Nothing about them should be harmful, physiologically unbalanced, or called into question regarding their conduct, their mental awareness, or their personality performance.

God's people are whole in mind, in motive, and in spirit. Are you sound?

Less Preoccupied. More Desensitized

Desensitizing trivia means being less preoccupied with yourself. Let the self, the sensitized self whose eyes are turned into itself, always check to see if it is functioning properly; let the old confused thing alone. Desensitizing yourself to yourself is sensitizing yourself to Christ. The less you are caught up with questioning yourself, the more you discover the greater quest for Christ.

The surest way to be free from unfounded guilt or tantalizing fear is to become deeply aware of the Holy Spirit in your life. The deeper the self indulges in itself, the less the self indulges in the Spirit. The greater you seek to follow the principles of holiness, the less you are aware of holiness. Self is self whether it is in the religious world or the secular world. Christ did not come to kill the self; He came to fill it with Himself. The self, then, once filled with Christ, functions as in the original purpose of creation.

I was having coffee one morning, mentoring a young doctor. He said, "I am trying to make God part of my business." I said to him, "He will never be part of your business. He is your business. You and He are one." Jesus said that He is the vine and we are the branches, meaning that the life in the vine is the same substance in the branch that produces the fruit. One substance.

There are no parts or divisions in God. There are degrees of knowledge of God, but there are no degrees of having God. Being filled with the all the fullness of Christ is simply being filled with all the revelations of God unfolding to you, which are endless. Some people seem to have more of God than others. That is an illusion. They just have a better understanding of God and, perhaps, have yielded more to His leadership.

Having more of God is having the capability or the capacity to receive more of God. The bigger the glass, the more water it holds. In like manner, the greater the depth of the soul or the enlargement of the inner man, the greater capacity there is for the indwelling of God.

God is a Spirit. You are a spirit. Spirits join only when they possess the same quality or substance that blends. He is the substance in the branch. He is the substance in the vine. All you need to focus on is the enlargement of your spirit to flow in the substance.

The greater your spirit, the greater the possibility of the Spirit in you. How full are you? A developing spirit is enlarging for the fullness of His Spirit.

What size is your spirit?

Thinking through His Mind

You have the mind of Christ (1 Corinthians 2:16). What would you think if a world famous psychologist or psychiatrist said, "You have the mind of Einstein"? What would happen to your self-image and your abilities to achieve your greatest goals if you accepted this statement as true? There would come to your mind the enthusiastic thought, "I can do anything I set out to accomplish. I have the mind of Einstein!"

Yet you have been informed that you have the mind of Christ. How does that affect you? Let His mind think through yours, and let your mind think through His.

When Jesus said, "…if my words abide in you…," He was using the word *rhema.* At another time, He said, "You are clean through the word I have spoken to you." That word is *logos. Logos* informs you of God; but the *rhema* infuses and empowers you with God. *Logos* deals with the reason. *Rhema* deals with the revealed.

You have the rhema-mind of Christ!

This is the concept of flowing in the mind of Christ while using your own mind. Everyone is seeking greater knowledge: how to build a business, how to build a church, or how to raise a family. They are running to every seminar, every crusade, reading every book they can buy, and yet, they seem to fall short of their goal. Why? It is because they are looking to be informed instead of being infused with the *rhema or logos* of God. None can give you what you already possess…the mind of Christ. Learn to draw on that mind. *Logos* leads to the rhema.

John said, "…ye have an unction from the Holy One, and ye know all things" (1 John 2:20). It is the unction—the anointing of the Spirit— which teaches you all things you need to know in your pursuit of living. Let me give you a simple illustration:

Ruth Ann, my dear wife, came to me in desperation and said, "Don, I have been looking for a book that I love. I want to give it to Rick (our son-in-law) for his birthday." She had searched the house, but no book! In that moment, I went into the mind of Christ. I said to her, "You will find the book in the next fifteen minutes."

She walked down the stairs, and to her jubilant surprise, there was the book on top of our old grandfather clock. With the mind of Christ abiding in the Spirit of Christ, I was able to help her find the book.

What are you looking for? What do you need in searching for a job? Find the answers in the rhema or the mind of Christ. It is in you. Act as if you have the mind of Christ. His mind in you is more than just your salvation. It is your victorious lifestyle of making a life, too.

PART FOUR

The Devil Intimidates

Devils are intimidators. They use words of accusation in seeking every possible way to shame you. The purpose is to make you timid or fearful of yourself or your work. It keeps the mind in uncertainty, making it impossible for God to use you in a mighty way. Your daily work suffers loss if the devils win in their intimidation against you.

No doubt, you understand this spirit of intimidation. It seeks to cow, or browbeat you with a sense of inferiority.

Demons demand more than you can live or give.

They use threatening, insulting, and bullying ways against you, in hopes of you giving up your faith, your ideas or ideals, and your inner self-image. Devils are arrogant, scornful, and contemptuous in treating your walk or work with Christ—browbeating you into submission, contradictions, and confusion.

Devils use your natural weaknesses against you—seeking to convince you that you are not in the league of the great. Others may live and walk in this league, but not you. The devil sends mixed messages. The great trick is to have you second-guess yourself. Second-guessing yourself stymies your best efforts.

After you have taken a step of courage, Satan forces fear into your mind. Believing this lie cuts the joy, your physical strength, and your self-confidence. And it leaves you tossed by the waves of fear.

2 Timothy 1:6-7 reads, "… I put thee in remembrance that thou stir up the gift of God, which is in thee by the putting on of my hands. For God hath not given us the spirit of fear; but of power, and of love, and of a sound mind."

The spirit of fear involves self-doubt, a sense of being wrong, undue strain in circumstances, and emotional uncertainty. To put this spirit of intimidation to death, which stymies your best efforts, is to stir up and rekindle the Spirit's fires. Rekindle the gifts of the Spirit and the miraculous power in you if you want to win over the spirit of fear.

Intimidation is a spirit of fear. You must overcome it or it will overcome you. Are you an overcomer?

Understanding Two Ways

You are seeking to know the ways of God versus the ways of Satan. Both are vital to your welfare. Seek not to be ignorant of the devices or wiles of Satan, but be equally knowledgeable of the ways and the deliverances of God. There are two ways, two methods, two voices, two spirits, and two insights. There is the spirit of truth and the spirit of error.

Knowing this truth brings great miracles and marvelous insights into the unseen world. What you know about the unseen world will affect what you experience in the visible world. Romans 4:17 declares, "…God calleth those things which be not as though they were."

Satan is a terrorist. He works undercover until he gains the upper hand.

He moves among us acting as us, while hiding his identity and his true intentions. He hopes to make the world, the flesh, and evil seem harmless. He takes your purity and seeks to lead you into fanaticism. He fights on your ground, seeking to take your most protected areas and turn them into a door of entrance and entanglements. Your strongest points become his weapons, attempting to turn your strength into confusion or unfounded convictions, hoping you will give into his bullying.

Demons deal and torment in the details . . . the trivial areas of life. The purpose of this trick is to take your focus from the big things or the most vital things in your faith. If he can get you trying to catch the minnows, then the sharks will eat you! The great opportunities will go right by you, while your eyes are on the minnows or focusing on the pebbles at the beach. The zeal in which you look for the small—the insignificant—is the zeal going to waste.

Satan is not only a terrorist. He is also a destructor.

It has been suggested that God deals with details, not with generalities. Yes, He does deal with details, until you learn the trick of them and discard them. However, God has a world to reach, a soul to develop, and a spirit to fill. He dips your mind, your soul, and your spirit, along with your ambitions, into the depths of the ocean of faith, hoping you will learn to swim among the sharks while not being eaten by one.

When you go for the big things of faith, it is amazing how all the small things of faith follow. Go for the other shore and see the miracle of Jesus walking on your storm-water.

I'm Sick of It

My son woke up one morning and said these words: "I'm sick of those who keep trying to change me, and see no need to change themselves. I'm sick of people telling me what to do. I'm sick of associating with religious minds that end up in religious clubs."

"I'm sick of failures propping themselves up as winners with other people's names, books, and businesses. They don't have enough in themselves without being propped up by other's achievements."

"I'm sick of being pulled down emotionally so that others can feel superior."

"I'm sick of making excuses why God doesn't move, touch, heal, prosper, and give peace in the storm. After all, He promised it. Let Him fulfill it. So be it."

I permitted BJ to express his bold thoughts to see how he carries them out to his satisfaction and usefulness. Time will tell if he won over his sickness. I'll watch with eager eyes.

Test the Ground

Satan is not only a terrorist. He is also nitpicker. He nitpicked on Adam and Eve. Out of all the millions of trees, animals, and types of vegetation, Satan picked on God's intentions with one little tree or fruit. The nitpicking caused Eve to distrust the love, the nature, and the intent of God.

Satan's plan is to nitpick your relationship with God and your own personhood within yourself. Distrust of yourself in the decisions you make causes your distrust of God in the decisions He makes. Distrusting yourself causes you to distrust God's care and His intentions for you.

God comes to help you with specifics in your walk. Satan comes with specifics to hinder you in your walk. He came to Jesus in the wilderness and brought up the specifics of food, fame, and security. The same tactics he uses today.

The nagging condemnation of the enemy focuses on some particular aspect of your life. He seeks to use the questionable particulars to hold you in fear, despair, and torment. As long as he holds your attention on the details, the particulars, your attention is off the greater matters as to what it is to love God with all your heart.

There are times when you will need to crash headlong into the test and prove if it is of God. The Scriptures urge us to test the spirits and see if they are from God. Is this the spirit of truth or the spirit of error? The call of the Scriptures is to test the spirits—to try them in an open challenge. Make them prove their point, scripture by scripture and experience by experience.

It would be just as sinful to walk in the spirit of error as to fail to walk in the spirit of truth.

You lost liberty and wholeness of mind out of self-doubt, double-doubt, and fear of consequences. You failed to remember that consequences are part of growing, learning, and winning in the walk of faith. God forgives consequences quicker than cowardice. What are you afraid of?

Work Out Your Deliverance

Philippians 2:12-13 urges, "Wherefore, my beloved, as ye have always obeyed, not as in my presence only, but now much more in my absence, work out your own salvation with fear and trembling. For it is God which worketh in you both to will and to do of his good pleasure."

Working *out* your salvation is not working *for* your salvation.

Your salvation, deliverance, and healing have been accomplished with Christ. Working it out is to discover all the benefits of that deliverance and make it good in practical daily living.

Working out is not physical only; it is spiritual and mental also. This kind of spiritual or mental work out is not just in youth. It is happening all your life. If you stop being actively creative in your mind, spirit, and your physical muscles, then they will refuse to respond. Unresponsive muscles die.

A friend called me on the phone, and in the conversation said, "You walk with God as if you were just saved. The zeal, the fervency, and the intensity reminds me of a person who just received Christ, but you have walked with Him for many years. Your enthusiasm for Christ and for His work never ceases." If this is true, then I have endeavored to keep the faith muscles, the spirit, and mind muscles exercised.

Working out the deliverance never ceases for the truly committed. "The zeal of thine house hath eaten me up," Jesus said of Himself (John 2:17). To be zealous is to be hot like the boiling of liquids. You already have the Ideal within, but running after it brings the manifestation of it in life.

There is one thing you must learn and relearn in the walk of revealed truth. Nothing is yours until you test it, take it, and use it for good. You are complete in Christ, but that completeness must be learned on the battlefield of living.

However, you will only seek and find what you know is yours.

If you fail to know, then you will fail to seek. And in failing to seek, you will not find the prize. Therefore, find out what God is saying about the things you are seeking. Find the truth about what you already posses. Knowing what is yours makes seeking it easier and receiving it quicker.

The Vulnerable Position

Many of our leaders pour guilt teaching or guilt instruction or scriptural faultfinding on their people, thinking this method will motivate them to action. But it works in the opposite way.

Satan is using this tactic already. He uses guilt-fear, pointing out the lack or need in the person. However, if spiritual leaders take the same approach, it only doubles the trouble-doubt of yourself or your acceptance with God. It leaves you in a vulnerable position.

That vulnerable position leaves you open to being violently and emotionally attacked by others or devils—with blows of painful words or images on the mind. It is literally opening people's minds to be damaged or wounded in spirit and emotions. Thus, the whole body of believers is weakened in spirit, in the prayer of faith, and most seriously, weakened in personal witnessing. The ideal is damaged again in them.

If the spiritual image is wounded or the faith ideal is damaged, then the whole personhood is cracked. If the personality is cracked, then you will feel like a double-person or triple-person in the psychic. The cracked personality is unsure which one is at the front doing the work. There is produced, then, a defective and dysfunctional, but sincere, believer. What a shame.

In this confusion, you are now convinced that this nagging voice is the true voice. You hear it from without, in the meetings, and you hear it from within, in your own mind and heart. It all must be true. Therefore, you fall into the age-old trap of self-effort: just try a little harder, do a little more, or be a little better. And then, out of your weakness, you fake it just to be accepted in the group.

Faking the faith is not something new. Faking wholeness brings on more sickness of mind. Nevertheless, to know or to accept the way out is too risky. It is taking the risk on all you have learned or experienced, and you may never get back to that safe place of bondage again! So you make the choice to fake it.

Oh, Lord, send someone to us who has the anointing of Luke 4:18! "The Spirit of the Lord is upon me, because he hath anointed me to:

(1) preach the gospel to the poor; (2) heal the brokenhearted; (3) preach deliverance to the captives; (4) recover sight to the blind; and (5) set at liberty them that are bruised."

The next time you are conned into faking it, try this approach.

Each Level Must Be Taken

I was taking my usual walk on a cool August morning. As I left the front door with my brass walking stick, I said, without thinking, "Lord, I'm as holy as you can make a man!" It rocked me! I was shocked to be so frank before the Lord (or so brass). I dared to go on and said more, expecting any moment to get a rebuke from the Spirit. But there was no rebuke or even a shadow on my heart.

I learned that I was not grieving the Spirit! With freedom, I went on to say, "Lord, I am as favored as you can make a man; Lord, I am as loved, as prayerful, as anointed, as disciplined, as accepted, and as beloved as you can make a man." With all of that said, I expected a hit over the head with a bolt of lightning. But nothing happened.

However, following these statements of faith, all hell broke loose in my personal life. The enemy came to test my true belief and confidence in these declarations. The attacks were so intense that I thought I would not live to see the next day. The inner man, my soul, and my spirit, were fighting for their very existence. The devil tested me with the heat of hell to see if I would let go of these declarations of faith. It took all there was in me to hold on until the victory was won. Every new piece of faith-ground must be declared, taken, and then held, if it is going to be yours permanently.

The truth of these statements of faith was so profound to my inner man that I repeated them to my wife when I arrived home from my brisk walk that fall morning. She said with a sweet twinkle, "Don, don't preach that. Don't tell anyone you believe that."

I knew right then and there that I had found a wonderful, life-transforming secret. If your best friend questions or overly cautions your newest secrets, it is a sign from the Lord and a test to see if you really believe what you found to be true. So here I am, writing it for the whole world to read!

You are the best God can make you, too, up to this point. Rejoice in that point of your journey while moving on to greater levels in God.

Cultivate the New You

It is essential you affirm the confession of faith in the new place, the new ground, the new knowledge, and the new freedom you found in Christ. Affirmation is the secret to continuation in the incredible walk.

Each new evidence of life, or each new evidence of freedom, must be affirmed if you are to continue to walk in liberty.

Each new evidence of freedom is to be learned by you for it to work its way out into the reality of living. The new thoughts need to be cultivated. Each new promise and each new insight to yourself (and of Himself) is to be understood for it to be useful. You will need again and again, repeatedly, to get acquainted with the new self, the new vocabulary, and the new freedom—if you are to be vigorous in your work of faith.

The new relationship level with the Father is essential to be understood. You have known the Father in bold regulations. Now you know Him in bold a relationship. Fresh revelation calls for fresh association. How do I walk, think, or respond to this new knowledge? How do I respond to this new self-image in God? What is the better method in doing the work of God, with this greater, cleaner knowledge and revelation of Christ in me?

In this new level, you will encounter greater conflicts. The concepts call for conflict. The concept in the mind—in the new image-freedom—brings on greater conflicts, questioning your new image in your walk of holiness. The inner man, having yet to unlearn his ways of bondage, will oppose your insistence of the new image and the new method of walking in the Spirit.

The unlearned inner man will insist that you retreat to the old fears. The inner mind will oppose your insistence of the new image. The inner mind will insist on you holding to the old familiar bondage. Why? Because it is more comfortable; and yet, it is miserable if you do so. It feels safe to the old self-image. Here is where the battle is joined. Do I press on against the familiar fears or do I give up the battle for unsafe peace?

I have heard the old, morbid, inner mind speak, like it was in the room, "If you don't stop this, you will lose your soul." The voice was loud, forceful, and very frightening to me. In that second, I turned to fear. It took some time to understand that the voice was not the voice of the Spirit. The Spirit does not threaten. There are no harsh tones or threatening tones in His voice. Nevertheless, being very sensitive, I took the voice to be the Spirit; the result was fear and dread. It took time for me to disregard the threat and stay in the war of winning. I made the voice prove itself. It failed. I won. I thank God that my type of disposition or temperament is to search for answers, and not be afraid to test the voices or the leadings of my own spirit. This very disposition has given me great advantages and much insight into the lives of many people, producing freedom and joy in their incredible walk, too.

Take the case of a minister who had been burdened for years with an obsession (which he thought was sin) only to find out in the end that his obsession was simply and purely subjective—without reality. His "new you" was discovered after struggling with morbid guilt for years. What a relief it was to his mind and emotions, making him much more effective and happy in his work.

Are you cultivating your "new you" concepts?

Old Attainments Oppose New Advancements

Your spirit will not take on new ways until it is awakened. The old attainments seem good enough to the sluggish man. Therefore, the inner self must be awakened and aroused to the possibilities of a better faith position if it is to advance to greater attainments. Once the greater position is seen by the inner man, then the possibilities are opened. What has been accomplished is seen with thanksgiving, but the new possibilities stir up the faith of the inner man for greater advancements.

The apostles found a new energy after Pentecost. They not only found a new energy, but they found a new self-image energy. With the new self-image and the new power of the Spirit, Peter and John could say to the cripple man at the Beautiful Gate, "Look on us" (Acts 3:4). This would seem to be arrogance. Instead, it was the old attainments passing away when they walked with Jesus, making room for the new release of power and new attainments.

The new advancement has to forget the old attainments if it is to reach the utmost. Who you were or what you have done is passing away for a better you and a deeper usefulness.

When you enter new ground or new territory, you will need to learn how to act or how to think if you are to work effectively with the new pinnacle or plateau. Now you are moving from the thought of faith, to the word of faith, and finally, to the reward of faith. What stage are you in?

Distinguishing the Voices

Isaiah declared, "Your ears shall hear a word saying, 'This is the way, walk in it, when you turn to the right hand, and when you turn to the left hand, you will hear the voice giving directions'" (Isaiah 30:21, *free translating*).

As it takes time for the new baby to learn the voice of the mother, distinguishing it from all other voices, so it takes time for the believer to learn the inflections of the Spirit's voice from all other voices, demons, or unbelieving voices. It is of the utmost importance that believers distinguish the voice of the dear Holy Spirit from all other voices, whether they are friends giving counseling or demons giving false signals.

In time, you will be able to distinguish the different voices by their sounds and by their effects on your emotions and spirit.

The voice of the enemy is unending chattering, and it rattles on and on. It is the voice insisting on the one subject or the one trivia, demanding an instantaneous response. It is a continuous flow of words and arguments, compelling an immediate response. Usually, it has to do with some form of negative limitation, or overly strict restraint.

The tone of the enemy's voice is harsh, demanding, and usually degrading. You are left with the feeling of being forsaken or lashed with whips. However, the voice of the Spirit is gentle. The tone is soft and intimate. It gives time for the believer to make a choice. The Spirit leads clearly, not forcing or driving the soul into the will or the presence of God.

It is actually possible to be forced into making a choice that seems holier, but in it, there is an impossible trap of condemnation.

Many people have lived in fear because of these unnecessary vows or commitments. Fearing the withdrawal of His presence, their lives are lived in dread, while seeking to maintain an unnecessary vow made to the Spirit.

The patience it takes in working out of a confusing situation is of the Spirit. The Spirit speaks in a word. He is not a running commentary. He does not need to go on and on to get your attention or to give you direction. One word will do for the loving, obedient child. The barrage of words is of the enemy.

There is no fear in love. And there is no love in fear. What do you love and what do you fear?

PART FIVE

You Have the Advantage

As a faith person, you have the advantage over the unbeliever.

Actually, you have two advantages over the unbeliever. The unbeliever uses only the natural mind, reasoning with life's obstacles while seeking to make a living and to build a life. But the Spirit-filled believer has both the natural and regenerated mind, plus the Spirit-ignited mind, while living and building a life by the indwelling of the Holy Spirit. You can't lose. The one follows the other in perfect harmony when understood.

You are assured of victory before you start, if you understand how to work with this truth. This assurance is not based on human facts, but on the revelational knowledge of the Spirit in your spirit. You have it as if it was parked in your garage.

At this point, it seems that you are invincible and undefeatable. A businessman used to speak of my ministry: "Whatever that guy does, works." I had a secret, which I was proclaiming every week. If he would have come to hear, he too would have the secret. It was a secret revealed.

The devils and those who oppose you are defeated before they know you are coming.

You will have the faith-working plans in your heart long before anyone will see them on the streets. How can you catch a faith-marathon runner if he started miles ahead? Devils don't know what the Spirit has put into the heart of the anointed. Before he knows it, the revival, the money, and the people are moved by the Holy Spirit to flow with your dream. Devils come along later, maybe in months or years, seeking to sidetrack the moving runner. He will never get it done if you stick with the original Spirit, which ignited your spirit in the move of God.

You know now what to do, not because you have studied it only, but because you have discerned it in the inner man. You have visualized it, vitalized it, and now you are verbalizing it.

Are all now experiencing what you have seen in your spirit?

Exaggeration Executes

Exaggerating the need or the results throws the situation out of focus.

Peter said to Jesus, referring to his fishing, "Master, we have toiled all the night, and have taken nothing: nevertheless at thy word I will let down the net" (Luke 5:5). "We have fished all night and have taken nothing." This was the response of exaggeration.

Peter's exaggeration never touched the faith-seeing eye of Jesus. All the others were convinced that Peter was correct. The sea is empty. Jesus responded as if He never heard Peter. There is a point of faith where you are not moved by the exaggeration of the need. "And when they had this done, they enclosed a great multitude of fishes: and their net brake" (Luke 5:6). The sea was not empty!

Follow the life of Jesus, and you will find that He encountered the exaggeration of need, repeatedly. For example, "By this time he is dead." "He has been dead four days." "You have nothing to draw with." "There is no way to feed this many people in the desert." "Why bother the Master?" "Come off the cross if you are the Son of God." None of these statements of urgency or exaggeration moved Jesus. He remained focused in His faith.

In most cases, Jesus had to put the ridiculing and the sobbing people out of the room before He touched the need. Peter, as well, put the crying women out of the room before he raised Dorcas from the dead (see Acts 9:40). These are emotional exaggerators. They kill faith. They exaggerate the need as bigger than the prayer of faith or the command of faith.

Once you know the facts, move toward the faith answer. If you allow the facts to dominate your mind, then you will submit to the problem. Hearing too much about the need, the problem, or the situation stymies faith. Understand the problem and ask what the need is, but immediately move to the possibilities of healing, deliverance, and victory.

All through the life of Jesus and the early church, the facts were stated with the expectancy of deliverance:

We have no food…go and see what's here.
The child is dead…believe only.
Caught in sin…go, and sin no more.
Peter kept in prison…but prayer was made for him.
The boat broke into pieces…they all swam to shore.
The serpent took hold of his hand…he shook it off in the fire.

The Scriptures endlessly compare need to supply. The faith-people could see through the need and the facts to the deliverance waiting to be experienced.

Death is swallowed up in life.
Sickness is swallowed up in wholeness.
Poverty is swallowed up in supply.
Darkness is swallowed up in light.
Mortality is swallowed up in immortality.

> "So when this corruptible shall have put on incorruption, and this mortal shall have put on immortality, then shall be brought to pass the saying that is written, death is swallowed up in victory" (1 Corinthians 15:54).

Are you comparing need against the prayer of faith?

PART SIX

Your Thought Is Your Talk and Your Walk

I have never been more convinced that what I think on is what I act on.

What I thought, I sought, and I wrought.

That statement is more than poetic in sound. The mind is the stimulation for all movement. There are many types of minds:

The emotional mind. The little mind. The searching mind. The business mind. The money mind. The praying mind. The creative mind. The perfect mind. The filthy mind. The negative mind and the positive mind.

It is vital that your mind be rewired when the wires of faith, hope, and trust have been cut by some trauma. Paul said, "…the inward man is *renewed* day by day" (2 Corinthians 4:16, emphasis mine). "… And be *renewed* in the spirit of your mind" (Ephesians 4:23, emphasis mine), and "…The new man, which is *renewed* in knowledge after the image of him that created him…" (Colossians 3:10, emphasis mine). To be renewed is to be restored, renovated, or refreshed in the spirit of the mind. "… [He] is able to do exceeding abundantly above all that we ask or think…according to the power that works in us" (Ephesians 3:20).

Take comfort, people of God, for what you thought you wrought, and your thought became your walk. God is working for us beyond what we ask or think. Again we are reminded, "For it is God which worketh in you both to will and to do of his good pleasure" (Philippians 2:13). But notice that it is both God and us working. We are to do along side of His doing.

God goes beyond your thought, at times, to fulfill what He desires for the "betterness" of your life. Notice there is only one letter difference between betterness and bitterness. However, that one letter makes all the difference. Your inner thoughts affect your attitude toward life, toward God, and toward the general path you are walking.

It is true. In the center of your being is the Spirit, the mind of Christ, and from that center, all thoughts float upward to your conscious mind, and out to your conscious world. There are times when your thoughts are not good, pure, or uplifting thoughts. But this is the tension, the battle of faith. Which thoughts will you allow to root? The root of thought is the fruit of the life.

Set your sails against the winds of hindering thoughts, for out of your thoughts, you are building the kingdom in which you live.

I Am a Slave

Since I am a slave, I have freedom. I have perfect freedom to perform as I am instructed.

My freedom is only limited by the boundary of my owner. Whatever He owns, I move over it to the fullest. The supply of my needs is not my responsibility. The One who owns me has the legal responsibility to supply my needs—to give perfect shelter and protection from invading thieves.

I am marked by His logo. When I buy, His mark on my hand gives the right to purchase to his account. I draw directly from His debit column. I am really a son-slave. When He took me from my previous position as a son-slave, I had no freedom. I had little hope—faint memories of some joy and pleasures, but it all seemed to hurt instead of help.

But, in a day, He came into the camp and took me out of it without the permission of my previous owner. I don't recall his asking my permission either. He just came and laid claim on me.

I followed, confused about what He had done—where we were going. I hardly knew who he was. He never answered me when I asked, "Who are you, and why are you taking me out of this old familiar camp?" I stumbled alone—walking behind him for some long time.

After awhile, and it seemed a long while, I began to understand that I was not my own, though I knew I was never my own. Someone always had ruled me. I never liked the ruler-ship, because it was dark, gloomy, and it had a sense of being dirty. I never learned much of life in that previous camp. However, I never knew there was a way out of this ignorance. No one had ever told me.

But His ruling had hope, and a measure of joy in it. The longer I understood his ownership, the more I knew the responsibility of being His. He would give orders, direction, and the ability to be a son-slave.

Instead of my ever seeking to become a son-slave, I began to realize that it was all done. He had the legal papers. I had the legal logo. It was done. I am now a slave who is free. I am free to be who I am and do as asked. But I yet fell into a bad habit of trying to make myself a perfect slave, while not remembering I am a perfect slave. A slave is a slave.

The secret is just remaining a slave. Let Him provide the bathing-house, the schoolhouse, and the counting-house. I began to understand that the becoming had come. I am what He says I am.

Faint Not

"And let us not be weary in well doing: for in due season, we shall reap if we faint not" (Galatians 6:9). Fainting is becoming weary in spirit and convulsing in heart. The mind falls apart when it faints. What is the answer?

The apostle Paul said that we faint not because of mercy. Watch for the mercy. Mercy gives a new beginning to the weary. It is like a heart-transplant, only it is a spirit-transplant. No doctor or hospital can give a spirit-transplant. However, the Spirit-anointed is able to transplant a new zest—a renewing of heart by the laying of hands or hearing anointed messages in the *rhema* of God.

You were born to battle. Nevertheless, the battle drains the soul. Winning the battles, though, puts zest in your work, and new zest in the daily routines of life. Paul said that we receive mercy. This is the life-tube for the soul.

Mercy is letting you up, letting you out, and letting you go…free.

As you become aware of the renewing of mercy, you are also aware of the winning attitude taking control. Repeatedly, God uses your struggles for you to grow, to succeed, and to overcome. He lets you up and lets you out.

The greater One brings you to your destiny. He brings about the outcome you were seeking.

The Plans You Make Mold You

Make your plans, but let your plans make and mold you. Pray your prayers, but let the prayers make and mold you. Write your book, but let the writing of your book make you greater than the book.

Let your work build you, while you are building the work. The worker must be greater than the work or the work perishes. The builder has more honor than what was built.

"… inasmuch as he who hath builded the house hath more honour than the house. For every house is builded by some man; but he that built all things is God" (Hebrew 3:3-4).

Your aim is to be greater in heart than what you preach. Seek to live better than what you teach or write. If you are not greater than your message, then the message is lost in emptiness. Many people have built a great business or a marvelous ministry, but in it, they lost their lives because they were not greater in heart than what they were doing. Your prayers must be bigger than your plans and greater than your desires if they are to bring the effect you are seeking.

If your plans are running you, they may in time ruin you.

There are some things, no matter how hard you try, that cannot be accomplished without a divine work. Give it all you got. However, in the end, it is the Spirit in your spirit that brings about the results. If you bring about the results, you will have to keep the results going. If the Spirit brings about the results, then He keeps the results going . . . long after you're gone.

The greater the attention you put on a matter, the greater attention the matter puts on you.

Once the wheels are set in motion and the prayers haven been prayed, let the prayers do their work through you. It may take months or years to accomplish the visionary-prayers, but in time, fervent faith will see the desires of the soul.

You are being presented each day an unscripted manuscript. The unanticipated confront you daily. How you handle these opportunities determines your destiny, your direction, and your inner divinity. If you run from or renounce these moments, then they will consume you in time. Face them head-on and you will win. The crowns are laid up for the winners.

Let no man take your crown. Let no system, let no bully, and no defeat keep you from your goals. You were created to win the prize. Blessings on you in your battle for success. God is with you!

The Lottery of Prayer

The word lottery is derived from the word "lot." Lottery is taking a chance, as taking a risk. Someone said, "There is no such thing as chance in our lives." I am not sure he is right. Prayer is always taking a chance. Everything you do in life has a risk to it. But the risk of taking the chance is a small price to pay for the sure dead-end street of the fearful.

The word "lottery" carries the idea of using lots, small stones, or short sticks to decide something among a group, an event, or an affair whose outcome is, or seems to be, determined by chance.

It seems that many pray as if praying the lottery. It is as if they are taking a risk or taking a chance to pray. The outcome is decided by chance, not Christ. Is this how most prayers are prayed?

We cast in the request, pull the lever, and hope it comes up a winner on the wheel of fortune. It is not much better than the Hindu pulling the prayer wheel. Hopefully, it stops on the desired answer.

While you have the promise of the answer, you also take the risk to pray. Not every time does the prayer have in it the certainty of the outcome. And, yet, it is very destructive to faith to insert the phrase, "Thy will be done," after offering a prayer. It is shifting the outcome over on God's side instead of maintaining the responsibility of faith on my side.

The will of God is the Word of God, and yet, in many details of life, there is no perfect word for the troubling situation. At a time like this, take the risk of faith. Cast the lots of faith, hope, and love with expectancy. Failing to take the risk is certain to take nothing off the altar.

If you risk nothing, it is certain you will receive nothing. How much are you risking for the greater answer?

The Lottery of Faith?

There is the general Word of God for the general ways of life, but specific answers take something more than a word or a promise in the Scriptures. Here is where the risk comes in. You face the need, and you take a chance that the need will be met when you pray. The outcome is truly in the mind of God and in the faith you exercised when praying.

And yet you must continue to ask, to knock, and to seek. Herein lies the mystery of prayer and faith. No one has the exact set of stones or set of sticks or set of cards to know the perfect outcome every time. However, you can be assured that the outcome of your praying will be in your interest, even though at times you are not able to discern it.

Before Pentecost, the apostles cast lots regarding who was to take the place of Judas (Acts 1:26). Before the outpouring of the Holy Spirit, the only method the church had in choosing their leaders was the lot or the vote—taking a risk. There was not much faith in it.

After Pentecost, the method was much more simple and direct. They said, when seeking the will of God, "It seemed good unto us, being assembled with one accord, to send chosen men unto you with our beloved Barnabas and Paul" (Acts 15:25). The main criterion was being assembled "with one accord." Being in one accord refers to being one in mind. There were no casting lots to find the Lord's mind. They seemingly knew the Lord's mind. And yet, there was the human element when they said, "…it seemed…"

Acts 16:9-10 gives a clear understanding in finding the will of God. It is like putting together a puzzle, as knitting the pieces in place for a clear pattern. "… a vision appeared to Paul in the night; There stood a man of Macedonia, and prayed him, saying, Come over into Macedonia, and help us. And after he had seen the vision, immediately we endeavored to go into Macedonia, assuredly gathering that the Lord had called us for to preach the gospel unto them."

The phrase "assuredly gathering" has the idea of working the puzzle of circumstances in finding the right course of action. They looked at all the possibilities in the circumstances, and made the decision from their puzzle to go. It was the Lord's mind; and they went.

Here is an additional puzzle regulating the requirements for the new believers. It was a problem to be solved by the apostles. The answer: "For it seemed good to the Holy Spirit, and to us, to lay upon you no greater burden than these necessary things" (Acts 15:28). The puzzle was solved by two necessities: "…it seemed good to the Holy Spirit…and it seemed good to us." In a simple stroke of submissiveness among the leaders came this undefeatable answer. The puzzle was solved, and the church moved on like a might army.

This is an example of the early church moving beyond the guessing, the risk taking, or the lottery method to find the rules and regulations for the early believers. How simple this method, and very effective. The amazing thing was how few rules they gave to the new believers, and how quickly the believers implemented them.

I am not going to suggest that we do away with voting or casting lots, but I leave it there for your consideration and thought.

What is your method in finding the will of God?

Don H. Polston:

BA, B. Rel., Indiana Wesleyan University

Master of Philosophy in Counseling, Emmanuel Baptist University

Doctor of Philosophy in Temperament Therapy, PhD, Carolina Christian University

Founder of *Sunnyside Temple*, Waterloo, Iowa, one of the largest Wesleyan churches in America

Founder of *The Life That Wins* television ministries

Inducted into *The Hall of Faith,* Indiana Wesleyan University, Marion, Indiana

Certified Temperament Counselor with the National Christian Counseling Association

Ministered on Trinity Broadcasting Network, 700 Club Network, and Praise the Lord Television Network

www.ingramcontent.com/pod-product-compliance
Ingram Content Group UK Ltd.
Pitfield, Milton Keynes, MK11 3LW, UK
UKHW041927190726
13854UKWH00003B/1485